THIS BOOK WILL MAKE YOU

CALM

THIS BOOK WILL MAKE YOU CALM

An Hachette UK Company
www.hachette.co.uk

Summersdale Publishers Ltd
Part of Octopus Publishing Group Limited
Carmelite House
50 Victoria Embankment
LONDON
EC4Y 0DZ
UK

www.summersdale.com

Printed and bound in China

ISBN: 978-1-78685-998-3

Substantial discounts on bulk quantities of Summersdale books are available to corporations, professional associations and other organizations. For details contact general enquiries: telephone: +44 (0) 1243 771107 or email: enquiries@summersdale.com.

THIS BOOK WILL MAKE YOU

CALM

summersdale

INTRODUCTION

Amid the hustle and bustle of today's world – when we're caught in a constant stream of noise, emails and notifications – it can be rare to find a moment of *calm*. Many of us are unable to switch off, even for a few moments, so we feel anxious and stressed. But tranquillity is within your reach: this book will help you to slow down, quieten your mind and take a few deep breaths every once in a while. As you gaze at these soothing pictures, take some time to marvel at the beauty of the natural world and allow yourself to get lost in the serenity of a secluded beach, an undulant sea or a gentle sunrise. So, whenever you need a dose of instant calm, pick up this book and escape to a world of peace and quiet.

BREATHE...

TAKE IT
SLOW

ALL MY
WORRIES
FLOAT
AWAY...

GO WITH
THE FLOW

EVERY BREATH
CALMS ME

I inhale positivity...
I exhale doubt

EVERY CELL
IN MY BODY
IS RELAXED

I LIVE IN
PEACE

*I choose to
see the beauty
in the world*

SERENITY AND
RELAXATION
FILL MY WORLD

I feel safe

and warm

I AM
CENTRED

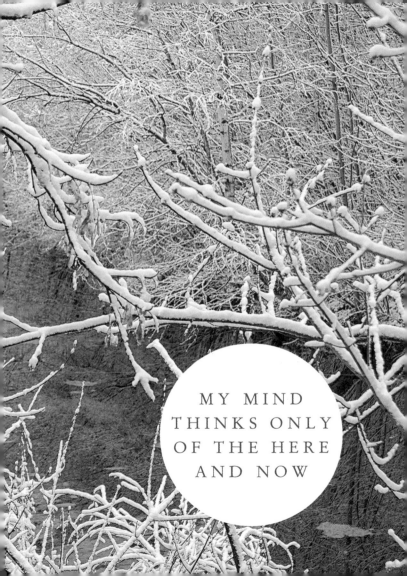

MY MIND
THINKS ONLY
OF THE HERE
AND NOW

THOUGHTS
COME
AND GO
LIKE BIRDS
GLIDING
ACROSS
THE SKY

THOUGHTS
COME
AND GO
LIKE BIRDS
GLIDING
ACROSS
THE SKY

ALL IS
WELL

I ALLOW
MYSELF
TO REST

MY MIND
IS STILL
AND CALM

Smile...

I CHOOSE
LOVE

I AM
CONTENT

MY MIND
IS MY
SANCTUARY

I am exactly

where I need to be

I LIVE WILD
AND HAPPY
AND FREE

CALMNESS
WASHES
OVER ME

I AM IN
HARMONY
WITH MY
SURROUNDINGS

Live in

the now

I AM AT
ONE WITH
THE WORLD

ENJOY THIS
MOMENT

I MATTER

ALL MY CARES
FLOAT AWAY
ON THE WIND

I TREAT
MYSELF WITH
KINDNESS
AND LOVE

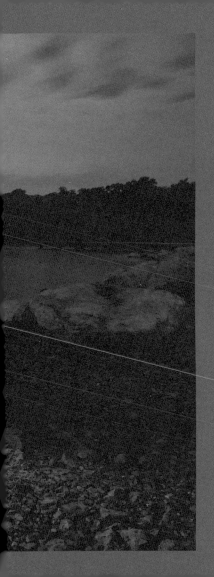

SURRENDER
TO CALM

MY MIND IS
AT EASE

I appreciate

myself

LET GO...

LIFE IS ON
MY SIDE

MY MIND IS
SLOWING
DOWN

I BREATHE
IN JOY

I LET GO OF
PAST CARES

EVERY DAY
I AM MORE
AND MORE
RELAXED

I FEEL
CALM AND
CONTENT

WARMTH
AND LOVE
SURROUND
ME

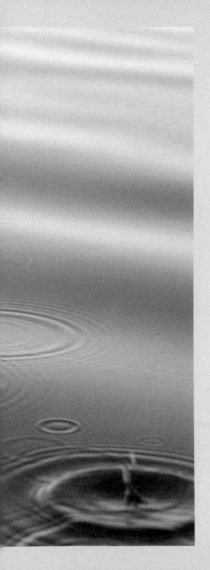

I SEE
THE JOY IN
EVERYTHING

MY LIFE IS
FILLED WITH
WONDER

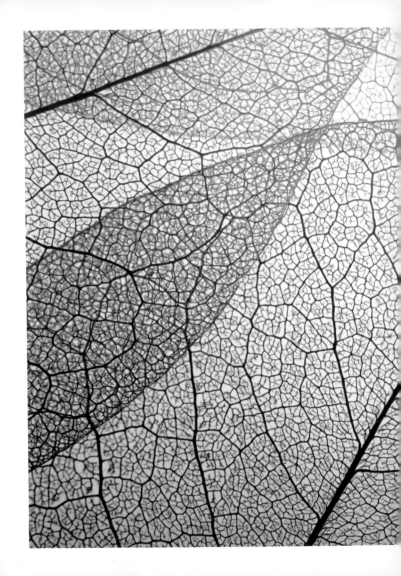

ALL IS
TRANQUIL

I SHED ALL
NEGATIVE
EMOTIONS

I let go of
anxiety and
embrace calm

TENSION
MELTS AWAY

I GREET
EACH
DAY WITH
POSITIVITY
AND JOY

I embrace

tranquillity

PEACE
SURROUNDS
ME

I FEEL
SOOTHED

I AM
FILLED WITH
GRATITUDE

My mind

is clear

ENJOY THE
STILLNESS

I welcome

serenity

Relax...

THERE IS
NOTHING
TO DO
RIGHT NOW
BUT BREATHE

Negative

thoughts

evaporate

I FEEL
COMFORTABLE

*I love and
am loved*

IMAGE CREDITS

If you're interested in finding out more about our books, find us on Facebook at **Summersdale Publishers** and follow us on Twitter at **@Summersdale**.

www.summersdale.com